Managing Editor
Ina Massler Levin, M.A.

Editor-in-Chief
Sharon Coan, M.S. Ed.

Illustrator
Sue Fullam

Cover Artist
Barb Lorseyedi

Art Coordinator
Kevin Barnes

Art Director
CJae Froshay

Imaging
Alfred Lau
James Edward Grace

Product Manager
Phil Garcia

Copyrighted materials and content reprinted with permission from Renaissance Corporate Services, Inc.

Publishers
Rachelle Cracchiolo, M.S. Ed.
Mary Dupuy Smith, M.S. Ed.

Practice Makes Perfect
Reading Comprehension
GRADE 3

Author

Teacher Created Materials Staff

Teacher Created Materials, Inc.
6421 Industry Way
Westminster, CA 92683
www.teachercreated.com
ISBN-0-7439-3333-8
©*2002 Teacher Created Materials, Inc.*
Reprinted, 2003
Made in U.S.A.

Table of Contents

Introduction

The old adage "practice makes perfect," can really hold true for your child and his or her education. The more practice and exposure your child has with concepts being taught in school, the more success he or she is likely to find. For many parents, knowing how to help their children may be frustrating because the resources may not be readily available.

As a parent it is also difficult to know where to focus your efforts so that the extra practice your child receives at home supports what he or she is learning in school.

This book has been written to help parents and teachers reinforce basic skills with children. *Practice Makes Perfect: Reading Comprehension* gives practice reading and answering questions to help fully comprehend what is read. The exercises in this book can be done sequentially or can be taken out of order, as needed.

After reading the story the questions can be answered either by circling the answers or by reproducing and using the fill-in answer sheets found on pages 46 and 47. The practice tests, for each of the areas of reading, can be bubbled in on the answer pages that are provided for each test.

The following standards or objectives will be met or reinforced by completing the practice pages included in this book. These standards and objectives are similar to the ones required by your state and school district and are appropriate for the third grade.

- The student will demonstrate competence in what is read.
- The student will demonstrate competence in understanding how print is organized.
- The student will demonstrate competence in using various reading strategies to read the stories and answer the questions.
- The student will demonstrate competence in finding the main idea in a story, making inferences and making predictions.
- The student will demonstrate competence in beginning to recognize different types of reading (fiction, nonfiction, informational).

How to Make the Most of This Book

Here are some useful ideas for making the most of this book:

- Set aside a specific place in your home to work on this book. Keep it neat and tidy with materials ready on hand.
- Set up a certain time of day to work on these practice pages to establish consistency, or look for times in your day or week that are less hectic and conducive to practicing skills.
- Keep all practice sessions with your child positive and constructive. If the mood becomes frustrated or tense, set the book aside and look for another time to practice with your child. Forcing your child to perform will not help. Do not use this book as a punishment.
- Help beginning readers with instructions.
- Review the work your child has done.
- Allow the child to use whatever writing instruments he or she prefers. For example, colored pencils can add variety and pleasure to drill work.
- Pay attention to the areas in which your child has the most difficulty. Provide extra guidance and exercises in those areas.
- Read aloud with your child and ask reading comprehension questions.

Happy Birthday

"Mary!"

Mary heard her mother's voice and walked to the top of the stairs.

"One minute," she said. She pulled her hair back and ran down the stairs. Mary walked past her mother, who was looking around impatiently. Mary knew that she would be late if she did not hurry, but she did not care. It was her birthday today.

Ten minutes later, Mary opened the car door and smiled over at her mother who said, "Now do not forget, you will go home with Cindy today." Mary tried to hide her disappointment. She had really hoped to have a party today, but her mother had to work late tonight. She promised Mary that they could have a party next week, but there was just something special about having a party on your birthday.

"I won't forget," Mary replied. She got out of the car and waved goodbye. It did not seem like her mother was very concerned. Mary walked quietly over to the school door and walked inside. She hoped her friends would remember that she was eight today.

"Hi Mary. Happy birthday," Julie said.

Mary smiled brightly and took out her pencils. "Julie, can you come to my party next week?"

Julie frowned and put her hand on Mary's shoulder. "I am sorry Mary, but I can't."

The rest of the day did not go much better. All of her friends said they could not go to her party next week. By the end of the day, Mary was fighting back tears on the way to Cindy's house. Cindy tried to cheer her up, but it was no use. Her big day was turning out to be awful. She could not wait until it was time to go home.

Evening came and Cindy's mother drove Mary home. Mary got out of the car and walked slowly to the porch, dragging her backpack behind her. When she opened the door, the house was dark. Her mom was not even home yet! Her shoulders slumped, and she turned to ask Cindy's mom to wait.

"Surprise!"

Mary spun around and all the lights in the house went on. Her heart was soaring as she looked around. Her mother and all of her friends were there! The coffee table in the living room was filled high with presents. Gleefully, she ran into the kitchen. Her mother had prepared her favorite meal, lasagna and breadsticks. Atop the counter sat a big chocolate cake that made Mary lick her lips in anticipation. The bubbly voices of her friends filled the room. Mary stood next to her mom and grabbed her hand. "Thank you!" Mary said, delightedly.

Happy Birthday *(cont.)*

Reading Comprehension Questions

After reading the story, answer the questions. Circle the correct answer.

1. At the beginning of the story, why was Mary's mother acting unconcerned about Mary's birthday?

    a. She did not care about Mary.

    b. She forgot that it was Mary's birthday.

    c. She did not want Mary to know about the surprise party.

    d. She was trying to give Mary a hint about the surprise party.

2. What made Mary lick her lips "in anticipation"?

    a. The chocolate cake

    b. The lasagna and breadsticks

    c. The thought of a birthday party

    d. The toast she ate in the morning

3. What is the mood of this story?

    a. First it is sad, then it ends up happy.

    b. First it is happy, then it ends up sad.

    c. The whole story is happy.

    d. The whole story is sad.

4. Why did Mary's shoulders slump when she arrived at home?

    a. She was always a lazy person.

    b. She was excited about the surprise party.

    c. She was sad because she thought that her mom was not home.

    d. Her backpack was very heavy.

5. In the last paragraph, what does it mean that Mary's friends' voices were "bubbly"?

    a. Their voices sounded like they were floating.

    b. Their voices sounded very happy.

    c. They were talking about blowing bubbles.

    d. Their voices were making bubbles.

Help Our Baby!

The crystal water was clear and blue. Caitlyn kicked slowly and the big rubber fins on her feet pushed her gently forward. She took in a deep breath of air from her scuba tank. She smiled as she watched millions of bubbles float upward when she let her breath go.

Caitlyn loved to dive. Her parents had let her take lessons last year. This year was her first trip to the ocean. She had been so excited! For three days, her family explored the coral reef. Caitlyn had already seen many beautiful things. Yesterday she saw a school of colorful parrotfish. She liked the delicate pink of the coral. There was no telling what she might see today.

Caitlyn waved at her parents, who were swimming nearby. They raised their hands, giving the OK sign. Then Dad put up both hands with fingers outstretched. Ten minutes more, Caitlyn thought. She nodded.

At that moment, Caitlyn saw a dark shadow pass over her in the water. She froze. Shark! she thought. She floated very still. More shadows approached. Caitlyn felt her heart pound. Then one shape swam right past her. They were dolphins! Caitlyn was so relieved that she let out her breath with a whoosh.

There were three dolphins. One was a baby. The two adult dolphins swam on either side of the baby. Caitlyn smiled. Then she noticed that the baby was bleeding. Caitlyn looked closely. A huge fishhook was stuck in the baby dolphin's side.

Slowly the two adult dolphins nosed the baby toward Caitlyn. 'What do they want?' she thought. Then she understood. They want me to help their baby!

Carefully, Caitlyn took the hook out of the baby's side. She pressed her hand against the wound to stop the bleeding. Soon the baby wiggled out of her hands and swam back to its parents. The two adult dolphins looked at the place where the hook had been. Caitlyn heard the dolphins make high-pitched clicking noises at each other.

The biggest dolphin turned and swam toward Caitlyn. The dolphin nudged her gently with his nose. Caitlyn suddenly realized, "He's saying thank you!" Then the three dolphins disappeared into the blue water as silently as they had come.

Help Our Baby! *(cont.)*

Reading Comprehension Questions

After reading the story, answer the questions. Circle the correct answer.

1. Why is Caitlyn underwater?

    a. She fell off a boat.

    b. She is scuba diving with her parents.

    c. She wants to rescue dolphins.

    d. She is learning how to swim.

2. The first paragraph answers which of the following questions?

    a. Why does Caitlyn's dad tell her that she has ten more minutes?

    b. When did Caitlyn learn to dive?

    c. Why does the baby dolphin have a fishhook in its side?

    d. Where is Caitlyn when the story begins?

3. How did Caitlyn probably feel at the end of the story?

    a. Scared that the dolphins will hurt her.

    b. Puzzled about what the dolphins were doing.

    c. Eager to stop diving.

    d. Glad that she was able to help the baby dolphin.

4. What is the main idea of this story?

    a. Caitlyn helps a baby dolphin.

    b. Caitlyn's parents are diving.

    c. Caitlyn thinks that it is beautiful underwater.

    d. Baby dolphins are cute and helpless.

5. A good way to find out more about scuba diving is to—

    a. watch a television show about dolphins.

    b. ask somebody named Caitlyn.

    c. look up information about it on the Internet.

    d. learn how to fish without hurting dolphins.

The Fawn

Sara and her father planned a hike up a mountain trail near their home. The trail they chose began at the foot of the mountain and led all the way to the top. Sara had packed lunches earlier that morning. Her father filled their backpacks with other supplies and they were off!

As they started up the trail, Sara's father pointed out many different plants that lined the trail. He showed Sara the difference between the leaves of an aspen tree and the needles of a spruce tree. Sara was glad that her father knew so much! She always learned something whenever they went on a hike.

"Look over there," Sara whispered suddenly. They had just turned a corner on the mountain trail. Lying in the grass next to the trail was a small baby deer, or fawn. It looked at them with wide eyes, but it did not move.

"Where is its mother?" Sara wondered aloud. "Do you think we should stay here and watch it?"

"That's a good idea," answered her dad. "We must not go any closer, though." As they sat down and unpacked their lunch, Sara asked her dad why they couldn't go any closer to the fawn. He explained that sometimes, if the mother smelled humans too close to her baby, she would be too afraid to come back. Sara and her father agreed that they would wait for the mother to come back, but that they would not get too close to the fawn.

Soon a larger deer walked slowly up to the fawn nestled in the grass. After a few quick sniffs and a cautious glance at Sara and her father, mother and baby ran quickly down the trail.

Sara and her father packed up their supplies and continued up the mountain. They knew that the fawn was now safe.

The Fawn (cont.)

Reading Comprehension Questions

After reading the story, answer the questions. Circle the correct answer.

1. How does Sara's dad probably feel about the fawn?

    a. He wants to ignore it.

    b. He cares about its survival.

    c. He doesn't want to help it.

    d. He wishes he could be one.

2. What is the main idea of this story?

    a. There is a hiking trail near Sara's house.

    b. Sara's dad teaches her about trees and plants.

    c. A mother deer returns for her fawn.

    d. Sara learns a lesson from her dad while on a hike.

3. What is a good word to describe Sara's dad?

    a. Wise.

    b. Boring.

    c. Funny.

    d. Strict.

4. After this experience, what would Sara probably do if she were by herself and saw another fawn?

    a. Run up to it.

    b. Watch it from a distance.

    c. Feed it.

    d. Teach it about trees.

5. How will Sara's dad probably feel about her after the hike is over?

    a. Proud.

    b. Angry.

    c. Puzzled.

    d. Sad.

Mike the Cat

Mike the cat was an ordinary cat. He had two ears, four paws and a short, stubby tail. Wait a minute! A short, stubby tail? All the other cats that Mike had seen had long tails. Some tails were fluffy and some were not. But they were all long. Mike decided that his short tail would never do. He had to get a long tail! But how?

Mike traveled far and wide, trying to find a long tail. Along the way, he spoke with many cats that had long tails. "My, what an unusual cat you are!" they would say. "We have never seen a cat with a short, stubby tail." The cats would gather around Mike, asking all sorts of questions about what it was like to have a short tail. Mike often found himself talking into the wee hours of the morning, telling stories of how he could sleep in front of warm fireplaces, never having to worry whether someone was going to step on his tail. Or, about the times that he slipped out the backdoor and spent sunny afternoons chasing squirrels, when the slamming door would have caught other cats by the tail. It wasn't long before Mike became something of a celebrity! Other cats came to him to hear his amazing stories.

Soon, Mike forgot that he had left home in order to find a long tail! Maybe being a cat with a short, stubby tail wasn't so bad. Because of his unique quality, Mike had made many friends. "I guess being one-of-a-kind is not so bad after all," Mike thought. " I think I'll keep my short, stubby tail."

Mike the Cat *(cont.)*

Reading Comprehension Questions

After reading the story, answer the questions. Circle the correct answer.

1. Why did Mike decide that his short, stubby tail wasn't so bad?

   a. He was tired from traveling far and wide.

   b. He had made new friends because of his strange tail.

   c. He saw how other cats wanted to have his kind of tail.

   d. He didn't like the longer tails of the other cats.

2. What is the main point of this story?

   a. Being different is not so bad after all.

   b. The only way to have friends is to be different.

   c. No one should be teased for being different.

   d. It is important to be like everyone else.

3. What does it mean that Mike became "something of a celebrity"?

   a. Mike became popular because of his stories about his unusual tail.

   b. Mike starred in cat food commercials.

   c. Mike stood out because of his long, fluffy tail.

   d. Mike wanted to be the most popular of all cats.

4. What is Mike likely to do next?

   a. Find out how he can grow a longer tail.

   b. Find another way to be unique.

   c. Encourage the other cats to have short tails.

   d. Be happy with his short, stubby tail.

5. Why did the other cats gather around Mike?

   a. To ask him questions about his tail.

   b. To take pictures of Mike's tail.

   c. To find out how they could have a tail like his.

   d. To ask him why his tail was long and fluffy.

The Wood Carver

Ever since Greg was a toddler, he had watched his grandfather carve the small wooden figures. Greg was fascinated with the quickness of his grandfather's fingers as he switched the carving knife from one hand to the other, breathing life into what was once a lifeless piece of wood. Greg often wished that he could create wonderful little wooden figurines as his grandfather did.

One day, Greg's grandfather called the boy into the workshop. "Today is the day that you begin to learn the lost art of carving." Greg couldn't believe his ears as he pulled up a small stool next to his grandfather's workbench. The sharp smell of the wood filled his nose, and he moved in closely to where his grandfather was working. Greg's head was soon reeling with the names of the different tools his grandfather used to create the wooden treasures.

After the introduction to the tools was complete, Greg picked up a piece of wood to make his first attempt at carving. He loved the feel of the rough wood biting into his fingers. He worked for hours that day, trying to duplicate his grandfather's skill. Although his small, wooden figurine was far from perfect, both Greg and his grandfather were quite proud of the work Greg had done. "This piece will occupy a place of honor on my shelf," Greg's grandfather told him. Greg's eyes shone with joy. He knew that it would take many years to become as skillful as his grandfather, but Greg was going to enjoy every minute of it!

The Wood Carver (cont.)

Reading Comprehension Questions

After reading the story, answer the questions. Circle the correct answer.

1. How did Greg feel when he watched his grandfather carve wood?

    a. Worried that his grandfather would cut himself.

    b. Frustrated that he couldn't carve like his grandfather.

    c. Angry that his grandfather wouldn't teach him how to carve.

    d. Amazed by his grandfather's skill.

2. What will Greg probably do now that he's had his first lesson?

    a. Keep working on it to get better.

    b. Give up because he isn't as good as his grandfather.

    c. Throw out his first figurine.

    d. Chop down a tree in order to get some wood.

3. Why did Greg's grandfather put Greg's wooden figure on the shelf?

    a. Greg's grandfather knew it was not a good piece of work.

    b. Greg's grandfather was proud of Greg's first wooden carving.

    c. It was the best wood carving Greg's grandfather had ever seen.

    d. That is where Greg's grandfather always put the wooden figures.

4. Why did Greg's grandfather call wood carving a "lost art"?

    a. Not many people carve wood by hand anymore.

    b. Carving wood was done only by lost people.

    c. No one knows how to carve wood.

    d. There are no books about carving wood.

5. What does it mean to "breathe life into" a piece of wood?

    a. Greg's grandfather would make hollow wood pieces like whistles.

    b. Greg's grandfather could make a real-looking figure out of a piece of wood.

    c. Greg's grandfather always blew on the wood before he carved it.

    d. Carving wood could turn a dead piece of wood into a living one.

Square Dancing Llamas

"Swing your partner, do-si-do!

Now turn to the left and don't let go!"

This is the kind of song that professional square dance "callers" sing. It's the caller's job to sing out instructions during a square dance. Then the dancers do whatever the caller tells them to do. Callers need to have strong, clear voices so that the dancers can understand them. Professional square dance callers keep the dances interesting by coming up with new and funny things to sing.

One caller got to sing for some very unusual dancers. Tom Barry had been a square dance caller for many years. One day, he got a telephone call from a woman named Bea Kesling. Bea asked Tom if he would sing calls for llamas. At first, Tom thought Bea was talking about a dance club called the "Llamas." When she told him she was talking about dancing animals, Tom thought the idea sounded great. He said he'd do it.

Bea knew all about training llamas. Tom "called" while Bea and her friends gave dance lessons to eight of the animals. Bea made the llamas dancing outfits. She dressed them in colorful ribbons like those worn by women square dancers. Each llama danced with a person who guided the animal through the steps. Bea usually danced with a pretty yellow-haired llama she nicknamed "Goldilocks." The llamas were quick learners. It wasn't long before they were ready to dance in public.

Their first dance was for some llama ranchers in Lexington, Kentucky. The ranchers knew that llamas were smart and friendly, but they had never seen llamas dance. They didn't know what to expect. The dancers formed a circle and waited for Tom to start his calls. Tom called and the llamas danced perfectly. Everyone was impressed. The show was a big hit. Tom had succeeded at something no one had ever tried before. Since then, the llamas and Bea have kept dancing to the voice of Tom Barry, the world's first llama square dance caller.

14

Square Dancing Llamas *(cont.)*

Reading Comprehension Questions

After reading the story, answer the questions. Circle the correct answer.

1. Why did Bea Kesling call Tom Barry?

    a. He is a llama trainer.

    b. He is a square dance caller.

    c. He is a square dancer.

    d. He is a costume maker.

2. Who were the first people to see the llamas dance?

    a. Zookeepers

    b. Bea's friends.

    c. Llama ranchers.

    d. A group of square dance callers.

3. What is another good name for this passage?

    a. "Baby Llamas and Their Trainers."

    b. "Callers Who Care."

    c. "Goldilocks the Yellow-Haired Llama."

    d. "Swing Your Llama, Do-Si-Do."

4. How did Tom probably feel at the end of the passage?

    a. Sad.

    b. Angry.

    c. Proud.

    d. Hot.

5. A good way to answer the question just before this one is to—

    a. notice that Tom Barry did something unusual.

    b. notice that the llamas wore colorful costumes.

    c. notice that the llamas danced perfectly.

    d. think how you would feel if you watched llamas dancing.

Shirley Temple

Did you know that in the 1930s the most popular movie star in Hollywood was seven years old? Shirley Temple was a beautiful little girl. Her curly golden hair, bright eyes, and dimples were famous. She was a good actor, dancer, and singer.

Most importantly, however, she was able to show characters who were cheerful and brave. At that time, many families were out of work.. Nobody felt very certain about the future. But when Shirley Temple came on the movie screen, her positive attitude made people forget to worry, at least for a little while.

From 1932 to 1942, Shirley Temple made over 40 films. Some of the most popular were *Little Miss Marker, Curly Top, Heidi, Bright Eyes,* and *The Little Princess.* In 1934 Temple was given an Oscar for her special contributions to the world of film. Because she was still a small child, she was given a child-size version of the regular Academy Award.

By 1942 Temple was thirteen-years-old and no longer so small. She was changing, becoming a teenager. The country was changing, too. Because the United States was engaged in World War II, there were suddenly many jobs that needed to be done. More and more people were working, doing the jobs that had previously been done by people now away fighting as soldiers. People no longer had time to watch the golden curls and dimples of Shirley Temple.

Temple continued to act regularly in films until 1949, but none of these films were as popular as her earlier ones. At the age of twenty-one, she retired from acting. Soon after that she married a man named Charles Black. He was one of the few people she had ever met who had never seen any of her movies.

Although she occasionally returned to the world of show business, Shirley Temple, now Shirley Temple Black, concentrated on making her mark in politics. She was a delegate to the United Nations, where she was very involved in helping people from other nations.

Throughout her life, she has been very lucky. She has enjoyed wonderful adventures, fame, and riches, but she has given back to the world, too. First she cheered up a nation as a child; then she helped people and international relations as an adult.

Shirley Temple (cont.)

Reading Comprehension Questions

After reading the story, answer the questions. Circle the correct answer.

1. What is the main idea of this passage?

    a. Shirley Temple was one of the greatest child actors the world has seen.

    b. Shirley Temple has spent much of her life helping many people.

    c. In the 1930s, Shirley Temple was Hollywood's most popular actress.

    d. Child actors have always been successful at cheering up the nation.

2. Which of these is not a Shirley Temple film?

    a. *Dimples*

    b. *The Little Princess*

    c. *Bright Eyes*

    d. *Curly Top*

3. According to the passage, how did Shirley Temple "cheer up" the nation?

    a. She married a handsome man named Charles Black.

    b. She won a child-sized Academy Award in 1934.

    c. She helped people from other nations as a delegate.

    d. She was a talented actress with a positive attitude.

4. What did Shirley Temple do after she retired from acting?

    a. She continued making films, none of which were very popular.

    b. She made her mark in show business and earned an Oscar.

    c. She was a delegate who improved international relations.

    d. She helped cheer up families who were out of work.

5. By 1942 people no longer had time to watch Shirly Temple because

    a. she had made too many movies.

    b. the country was changing and there were jobs to be done.

    c. she no longer had a positive attitude.

    d. she was about to retire.

Sky Pioneers

When they were young, Orville and Wilbur Wright liked bicycles. They designed and built their own bicycles. They also repaired their friends' bicycles. After they grew up, Orville and Wilbur opened a bicycle shop. In this shop they built the first airplane.

In 1896, Orville got very sick. His brother stayed home to take care of him. This gave Wilbur a lot of spare time. He read a story about gliders. Gliders do not have engines. Gliders fly on wind currents. People wanted gliders with engines so they could go faster and farther. No one knew how to build one, but many people were trying. It was like a race to see who could build the first one.

The glider story excited the brothers about flying. They decided to build an engine-powered glider. Wilbur wrote to a museum for information about flying machines. He read everything he could find about them.

Wilbur studied hard. He solved one important problem. Changing winds made early flying machines crash. Wilbur designed a glider with moveable wings. When the wind changed, Wilbur's new glider could tilt its wings the right way. This would keep it in the air.

The next year, the brothers built their first glider. Then, they built a wind tunnel. This sped up their work. In the tunnel, they tested the glider in different winds. When the glider had trouble moving in the wind, they rebuilt it to work better.

The brothers built two more gliders. They tested them both in the wind tunnel. They also tested them outside. Then they built an engine-powered glider. This was the world's first airplane. On December 17, 1903, the brothers flipped a coin. The winner of the toss would fly the plane. Orville won. That day he made the world's first engine-powered flight. The flight lasted 12 seconds. The airplane traveled 120 feet. This short flight changed the world forever.

Orville Wright   Wilbur Wright

Sky Pioneers *(cont.)*

Reading Comprehension Questions

After reading the story, answer the questions. Circle the correct answer.

1. Why did Orville fly the plane first?

    a. Wilbur was afraid that the changing winds could make the plane crash.

    b. Orville won a coin toss.

    c. Orville had just recovered from his sickness.

    d. Orville was a better pilot.

2. What important problem did Wilbur solve?

    a. He designed a glider that would hold two people.

    b. He designed a glider that could fly in the dark.

    c. He designed a glider that could tilt its wings when the wind changed.

    d. He designed a glider that could fly in the rain.

3. What type of relationship did the brothers probably have?

    a. They probably enjoyed eating meals together.

    b. They probably did not understand each other.

    c. They probably did not see each other very much.

    d. They probably enjoyed working together.

4. Why does the story end by saying, "This short flight changed the world forever"?

    a. People thought that flying was dangerous.

    b. This first engine-powered flight led to the development of modern airplanes.

    c. People no longer cared about bicycles.

    d. The world would now know who the Wright brothers were.

5. This passage was written to—

    a. explain that Orville got very sick in 1896.

    b. tell the story of the Wright brothers and the first engine-powered plane.

    c. tell the story of how Orville and Wilbur designed and built bicycles.

    d. explain that it is important that brothers work together.

To the Moon!

In 1969, three men in a small spaceship made history with a trip the world will never forget. The three men were Neil Armstrong, Edwin "Buzz" Aldrin, and Michael Collins. The mission was called *Apollo 11*. Their destination was the moon.

Thousands of people worked to send those men to the moon. The project took many years. The project was called the Apollo Program. The first Apollo mission, called *Apollo 1*, was a disaster. The spacecraft caught fire on the ground. But the project continued.

During later missions, the astronauts practiced flying their spacecrafts. They also practiced the tasks they needed to know so they could fly to the moon and land on it. On the *Apollo 8* mission, the astronauts flew around the moon. They were nearly ready for the first moon landing.

The rocket that carried the astronauts and their spacecraft into orbit around the moon was called the *Saturn 5* rocket. It blasted through space at 25,000 miles an hour. Even at that speed, it took four days to get to the moon. The *Apollo 11* mission used a special craft designed only for landing on the moon. It was called the "Eagle." The Eagle landed on the moon's surface on July 20, 1969.

Only two astronauts walked on the moon that day. Neil Armstrong was the first person to step onto the moon. Edwin "Buzz" Aldrin followed him. The astronauts brought cameras with them, and the whole world watched the landing on TV. Michael Collins stayed in the spacecraft and circled around the moon. It was his job to look after the spacecraft that would take them home. He had to make sure nothing happened to it!

Today, the words Neil Armstrong spoke when he stepped onto the moon are world famous. He said, "That's one small step for man, one giant leap for mankind." The dream of going to the moon had come true.

The astronauts performed many experiments while they were on the moon. They collected rock samples and took pictures of the area around their spacecraft. The astronauts left an American flag and a plaque where they had landed. The plaque has the words "We came in peace for all mankind" printed on it. The flag and the plaque are still there. Someday moon travel may be more common. If that happens, people might visit the site of the first moon landing. They might have their pictures taken next to the flag and plaque.

To the Moon *(cont.)*

Reading Comprehension Questions

After reading the story, answer the questions. Circle the correct answer.

1. How did the "Eagle" arrive at the moon?
    a. It flew there on its own.
    b. Neil Armstrong sent it there.
    c. It was carried by the *Saturn 5* rocket.
    d. It was sent there by satellite.

2. How many astronauts walked on the moon on July 20, 1969?
    a. One.
    b. Two.
    c. Three.
    d. Four.

3. The last paragraph tells you that—
    a. Michael Collins looked after the spacecraft that would take them home.
    b. the astronauts left some American objects on the moon.
    c. the *Saturn 5* rocket carried the first people to the moon.
    d. people first landed on the moon in 1969.

4. The writer wrote this passage to—
    a. explain how difficult it is to travel in space.
    b. explain that the first Apollo mission was a disaster.
    c. talk about the first trip to the moon.
    d. talk about Edwin "Buzz" Aldrin.

5. These boxes show some things that happened in the story.

The *Apollo 8* mission flies around the moon.		Neil Armstrong steps onto the moon.
1	2	3

Which of these belongs in box 2?
    a. The astronauts performed experiments on the moon.
    b. The *Apollo 1* mission was a disaster.
    c. The *Saturn 5* rocket carries the astronauts to the moon.
    d. Neil Armstrong said, "That's one small step for man, one giant leap for mankind."

The Moth Named for the Moon

Most moths we see are very small. They are usually either white or brown. There are many other kinds of moths, but they are more rare. One beautiful type of moth is called the luna moth. "Luna" means moon. Like many moths, luna moths fly at night. In the moonlight they sometimes have a glowing green color.

The luna moth is actually a pale green. It has four spots, one on each wing. These spots sometimes look like eyes. The spots, or "eyes," are green, brown, and white. The luna moth is very large. It has long, sweeping lower tail wings. Once you have seen a luna moth, you will always recognize another luna moth by the spots, or eyes, or by the shape of its long tail wings.

The luna moth begins its life as a caterpillar. When it is a caterpillar, it is striped with green and yellow, and it has spines on its back. The caterpillar eats the leaves of hickory, walnut, sweet gum, and birch trees. Some types of luna moth caterpillars eat poison ivy! When it is time, the caterpillar makes a cocoon where it lives until it turns into a moth.

You can tell a moth from a butterfly by looking closely at its antennae. A moth has soft, fuzzy antennae and a fuzzy body. A butterfly has antennae that look more like thin, dark wire. Moths are more visible at night. You usually see butterflies during the day.

In the United States, most luna moths live in the eastern part of the country. If you're lucky enough to live in this area, look into the moonlight at night and see if you can spot a luna moth flying around among the leafy green trees.

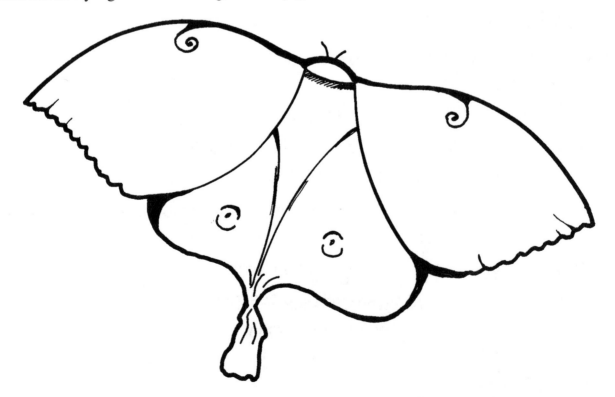

The Moth Named for the Moon *(cont.)*

Reading Comprehension Questions

After reading the story, answer the questions. Circle the correct answer.

1. When do luna moths sometimes have a glowing green color?
    a. In the sunlight.
    b. In the moonlight.
    c. When they live in the eastern part of the country.
    d. When they are very small.

2. What are the spots on the luna moth's wings called?
    a. Fuzzies.
    b. Antennae.
    c. Eyes.
    d. Wings.

3. You can tell that it is unusual that—
    a. some types of luna moth caterpillars eat poison ivy.
    b. the luna moth flies at night.
    c. most moths are very small.
    d. the luna moth has soft, fuzzy antennae.

4. What is the main idea of this passage?
    a. "Luna" means moon.
    b. Luna moth caterpillars eat different types of leaves.
    c. Luna moths live mostly in the eastern part of the country.
    d. Luna moths are unique and beautiful.

5. A good way to answer the question number 4 would be to—
    a. think about the different moths you may have seen in your life.
    b. look in an encyclopedia under luna moths.
    c. notice what most of the passage is describing.
    d. read what the last paragraph has to say.

Horses with Pull

Loggers have a tough job. Trees are big and heavy. They have to be hauled from hilly areas in the mountains. Trucks carry the trees to a mill to be processed. But these trucks can't drive on the winding dirt roads in the mountains. How do loggers get the trees out of the forest and onto trucks?

Many loggers use heavy machines to move and load logs. Logging machines are fast and very powerful. They have big engines and giant tires. But because they are so big, they can damage the forest. Big engines make a lot of noise and pollute the air. The large tires need wide roads to get in and out of the forest area and they can also trample delicate plants.

To solve this problem, some loggers have started using horses to move trees out of the woods. Horses don't have any of the problems big trucks and machines do. Horses are quiet. They also don't do as much damage to small plants or pollute the air.

So how do loggers use their horses to help them in the woods? First, the loggers cut the trees down. This is called felling. Then, the branches are cut off the tree and the trunk is chopped into short lengths. When the logs are ready, the horses are moved into position.

The logs are attached to the horses' harnesses with chains. When the horses hear the right command, they start pulling. Two horses can pull up to 1,500 pounds. This is about the same as the weight of a small car. The horses can pull the logs up to ¼ of a mile if necessary.

Loggers usually bring four horses to a job. That way, two horses can rest while the other two work.

Using horses for logging may seem old fashioned. Machines can do the job much more quickly and easily, but horses are better for the plants and animals in the forest. For this reason, many loggers have returned to this older way to work.

Horses with Pull (cont.)

Reading Comprehension Questions

After reading the story, answer the questions. Circle the correct answer.

1. Why have some loggers started to use horses?

    a. Logging machines cost too much.

    b. Horses are faster than logging machines.

    c. Horses can pull more weight than trucks.

    d. Horses are easier on the forest.

2. What is another good name for this passage?

    a. "Heavy Trees."

    b. "Horses are Strong."

    c. "Horses Replace Machines."

    d. "Horses Need a Break."

3. Which of the following can two horses working together haul?

    a. A small car.

    b. A locomotive.

    c. A truck.

    d. A big house.

4. The writer seems to feel that—

    a. using horses is more fun than using machines.

    b. using a machine is better when the logs are heavier than usual.

    c. using horses instead of machines is a good idea.

    d. getting the job done quickly is more important than anything else.

5. A good way to decide the correct answer for question 4 is to—

    a. think about the horses you have seen in your life.

    b. notice what the writer says in the last paragraph.

    c. read several books on logging.

    d. decide what your own opinion is about logging machines and horses.

Weird Weather

Weather does weird things. Air currents can raise the temperature of a city 100 degrees in just one day. Wind can lift heavy objects into the air. Sudden rainstorms can flood huge areas. Once in a while even stranger things happen.

For example, sometimes snow is pink. Snow forms in clouds high in the atmosphere. A strong wind may pick up red dirt on the ground. The dirt rises high into the air and mixes with the snow. When the snow falls to the ground, the snow looks dark pink. Pink snow is rare. Although people never see it, it does happen.

Even stranger things fall from the sky. One time, in France, it rained toads! It was a rainy day in a small town near Paris. The rain falling on the people's raincoats and umbrellas seemed normal. Suddenly, big, heavy toads started dropping out of the sky. The toads smashed windows. They bounced off people's heads. The people were very scared. It was a real mystery.

How can toads fall from the sky? Scientists have a simple explanation. They think waterspouts cause it. Waterspouts are tornadoes that form over lakes or oceans. Sometimes, a waterspout's strong wind lifts heavy objects into the air. The wind can even lift toads. A waterspout loses power when it moves over land. When this happens, whatever it lifted from the water falls to the ground.

Weather is hard to predict When strange things happen, they are difficult to explain. Remember this the next time you listen to a weather report. Don't be scared if the report says, "Watch out for falling toads in the morning. Pink snow with peas will fall by late afternoon!"

Weird Weather *(cont.)*

Reading Comprehension Questions

After reading the story, answer the questions. Circle the correct answer.

1. Why did toads fall from the sky?

    a. Waterspouts lifted them into the air.

    b. They fell from the clouds.

    c. Scientists do not know why.

    d. They fell out of airplanes.

2. Sudden rainstorms can—

    a. flood huge areas.

    b. pick up red dirt from the ground.

    c. smash windows.

    d. lift heavy objects into the air.

3. The first paragraph tells you—

    a. that weather is sometimes strange.

    b. that pink snow is rare.

    c. what waterspouts are.

    d. how toads can fall from the sky.

4. You can tell that the word "rare" means—

    a. uncommon.

    b. mysterious.

    c. sudden.

    d. pink.

5. What is the main idea of this passage?

    a. Air currents can raise temperatures.

    b. Snow forms in clouds high in the atmosphere.

    c. Weather can be unpredictable and weird.

    d. Toads are big and heavy.

How to Live in Death Valley

People use technology to live comfortably in hot climates. People use freezers to make ice cubes for cold drinks. They use air conditioning to stay cool. If they still can't stand the heat, they use cars to drive to a cooler place. One of the hottest places on Earth is Death Valley. The animals in Death Valley don't use technology to stay cool. But some of them have special abilities that help them live there.

Never Take a Drink!

The kangaroo rat is one animal that lives in Death Valley. It has big hind legs like a kangaroo, but it is really a rodent. During the day in Death Valley, it gets hotter than 100 degrees. The kangaroo rat rests all day in a hole in the ground. It plugs the hole with grass to keep out the heat. The inside of the hole stays cool from moisture in the

ground. The kangaroo rat comes out at night when the temperature is cooler. This little rat is also very good at conserving water. It gets all the water it needs from the foods it eats. Some kangaroo rats never take a drink of water in their entire life!

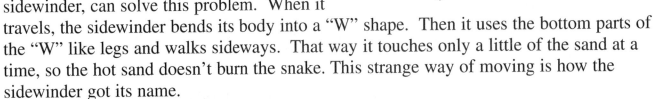

Don't Touch that Sand!

The sun makes the desert sand very hot. Animals, like snakes, get too hot if they lie on the hot sand too long. One snake, called the sidewinder, can solve this problem. When it travels, the sidewinder bends its body into a "W" shape. Then it uses the bottom parts of the "W" like legs and walks sideways. That way it touches only a little of the sand at a time, so the hot sand doesn't burn the snake. This strange way of moving is how the sidewinder got its name.

Drink Saltwater!

A lot of water in the desert is too salty for most animals to drink. All water has some salt in it. As the desert heat dries up pools of water, the salt is left behind. The remaining water in these pools can be three times saltier than the ocean. One kind of fish, the desert pupfish, can live in these salty pools because it can drink the saltwater. It gets rid of the salt through its gills.

Animals use their special abilities to live in Death Valley. People use technology to live in Death Valley. We use our imaginations to invent new tools. These tools keep us cool. Which way do you think works best?

How to Live in Death Valley *(cont.)*

Reading Comprehension Questions

After reading the story, answer the questions. Circle the correct answer.

1. Why do sidewinder snakes move in an unusual way?
    a. They are stronger than other snakes.
    b. They drink saltwater.
    c. They are avoiding touching the hot sand for too long.
    d. They spend all day hiding in a hole.

2. The purpose of the kangaroo rat staying in a hole during the day is—
    a. that it is scared of the sun.
    b. to watch over its young.
    c. to avoid the extreme heat.
    d. that there is food stored in the hole.

3. The first paragraph tells you that—
    a. technology is better than natural abilities.
    b. the pupfish drinks saltwater, and then gets rid of the salt through its gills.
    c. living in Death Valley requires special things for both animals and humans.
    d. different animals have different abilities.

4. You can tell that Death Valley—
    a. would be a good place to lie out in the sun all day.
    b. is a place where people cannot survive unless they drink saltwater.
    c. is a place where people would probably need special equipment to live.
    d. is a place where animals could not survive if it weren't for technology.

5. Why does the author include the last paragraph?
    a. To show how imaginations are helpful to animals.
    b. To contrast the way humans and animals survive in Death Valley.
    c. To explain why it is helpful to keep cool in hot places.
    d. To explain how the sidewinder moves.

Rainbow Soup

You can eat a rainbow if you put it in soup! Before you start, be sure to check and see if you have everything you need. And, most importantly, ask a grown-up to help with the stove!

Rainbow Soup

This recipe makes enough for two hungry people. You will need the following:

Rainbow Vegetables

$1/2$ cup celery, chopped into little bits

1 small carrot, cut into thin slices

1 medium-sized tomato, chopped

2 green onion tops, cut into small pieces

Noodles and Chicken

1 cup cooked multi-colored bow-tie noodles

$1/2$ cup cooked chicken, cut into tiny, bite-size pieces

3 cups chicken broth

Directions

1. Put the broth into a one-quart soup pot.
2. Add the rainbow vegetables to the broth. Do not add the onion tops yet.
3. Bring the broth to a boil.
4. Cover the pot with a lid and turn the heat to low.
5. Cook for 20 minutes.
6. Take the lid off of the pot. Add the rainbow noodles, chicken, and onion tops into the pot.
7. Simmer for 2–3 minutes or until the chicken and noodles are hot.

When the soup is ready, put it in a bowl. Now you and a friend can enjoy rainbow soup together.

Rainbow Soup *(cont.)*

Reading Comprehension Questions

After reading the story, answer the questions. Circle the correct answer.

1. What is the first step in the instructions?

    a. Cook the chicken.

    b. Put the broth into a pot.

    c. Put the noodles into a pot.

    d. Put the soup in two bowls.

2. After you cover the pot with a lid and turn the heat to low, how long should the broth cook?

    a. 2–3 minutes.

    b. 10 minutes.

    c. 20 minutes.

    d. 1 hour.

3. When will you need to add the noodles, chicken, and onion tops?

    a. After the broth begins to boil.

    b. After you put the broth into a one-quart soup pot.

    c. After the broth has cooked for twenty minutes.

    d. After the broth has simmered for 2 - 3 minutes.

4. A good way to answer the question right above this one is to—

    a. think about how long it takes water to boil.

    b. quickly skim over the recipe and directions.

    c. pay close attention to each step of the directions.

    d. look at a picture of the soup in a cookbook.

5. The directions in this passage are about how to—

    a. spot rainbows.

    b. enjoy soup with a friend.

    c. cook chicken.

    d. make rainbow soup.

Checking Out Books From the Library

Mark checked out a book from the library. Use this table of contents and index page from the book to answer questions.

Table of Contents

Index

Checking Out Books From the Library *(cont.)*

Reading Comprehension Questions

After reading the story, answer the questions. Circle the correct answer.

1. What is Chapter 3 about?
    a. Building a boat.
    b. Learning to sail.
    c. Rules for sailing.
    d. Caring for a boat.

2. Where can you find information about types of sailboats?
    a. Page 12.
    b. Page 37–39.
    c. Page 18–19.
    d. Page 14.

3. What would be a good name for the book that Mark checked out?
    a. Rescues of the Coast Guard.
    b. The First Sailboats in History.
    c. A Guide to Sailing.
    d. How to Build a Sailboat.

4. Why is Christopher Columbus probably included in the index?
    a. Because he sailed to America.
    b. Because he was Italian.
    c. Because he wrote the book.
    d. Because he liked sailboats.

5. The purpose of the index is to—
    a. make the book longer.
    b. tell you about the author's background.
    c. quickly find information in the book.
    d. rename the chapters.

Applesauce

Isabel has five friends. They are coming to her house for a snack. But she only has four apples. What can she do? She has a great idea. She can make applesauce!

Applesauce

Food You Will Need:

4 cooking apples

1/3 cup water

2 tablespoons cinnamon

3 tablespoons sugar

Equipment You Will Need:

vegetable peeler

2-quart pan with lid

cutting board

fork

sharp knife

potato masher

measuring spoons and cup

Directions

1. Peel the apples with a vegetable peeler. Put them on a cutting board. With help from an adult, cut the apples into four pieces and remove the cores. Throw away the cores. Put the apples into the 2-quart pan. Add the water and cinnamon. Put the pan on the stove.

2. With help from an adult, turn the burner to high heat. When the water boils, turn the burner to low. Put the lid on the pan and let the apples cook until they feel tender when poked with a fork. This will take eight to ten minutes. Turn off the burner.

3. With adult help, remove the pan from the burner. Take the lid off the pan. Mash apples with potato masher until they are almost smooth. Stir in the sugar.

4. Spoon the applesauce into dishes to serve warm, or cover with plastic or foil and then put in the refrigerator.

Makes 6 servings.

Applesauce *(cont.)*

Reading Comprehension Questions

After reading the story, answer the questions. Circle the correct answer.

1. What is the first step in the instructions?

    a. Prepare the apples to be cooked.

    b. Mash the apples.

    c. Put sugar on the apples.

    d. Cook the apples.

2. Why does Isabel want to make applesauce?

    a. She likes to cook with adults.

    b. It is her favorite snack.

    c. She has never made it before, and she wants to experiment.

    d. She needs to make a snack that will feed all of her friends.

3. It is a good idea to have a grown-up help you with cutting the apples because—

    a. knives are sharp, and you do not want to get cut.

    b. it is better to have someone else do the work.

    c. you might not cut the apple in enough pieces.

    d. grown-ups like apples a lot.

4. The core of an apple is the—

    a. center.

    b. sauce.

    c. recipe.

    d. peel.

5. The writer probably wrote this passage to show—

    a. that Isabel has five friends coming over.

    b. how to serve applesauce.

    c. how to make applesauce.

    d. that it is a good idea to get help from adults.

Hot Cocoa

Arturo and Carlos have been playing outside. They're cold, cold, cold! Their mother tells them to take a hot bath. Then she shows them how to make hot cocoa! Yum!

Hot Cocoa

Food You Will Need:

$^1\!/_3$ cup sugar

$^1\!/_3$ cup unsweetened cocoa powder

Dash salt

$^1\!/_3$ cup water

$3^1\!/_2$ cups milk

$^1\!/_2$ teaspoon vanilla

Equipment You Will Need:

$1^1\!/_2$-quart pan

measuring cups and spoons

wooden spoon

whisk

4 cups

Directions

1. In the pan, mix sugar, cocoa, and salt. Slowly stir in the water. Put pan on the stove. With help from an adult, turn the burner to medium heat. Cook and stir until the mixture boils. Boil one minute, stirring all the time.

2. Add the milk, one cup at a time, stirring as you do. Heat and stir until the mixture starts to bubble around the edge of the pan. Turn off the burner. With help from an adult, move the pan off the stove. Stir in the vanilla.

3. Use the whisk to beat the mixture until foamy. Be careful not to splatter it. Pour it into the cups.

Hot Cocoa *(cont.)*

Reading Comprehension Questions

After reading the story, answer the questions. Circle the correct answer.

1. When should you add the milk?

    a. After you stir in the vanilla.

    b. After the mixture has boiled for one minute.

    c. After you pour the hot cocoa into the cups.

    d. Before you add anything else.

2. When should you turn off the burner?

    a. After you use the whisk to beat the mixture.

    b. Whenever you feel like it.

    c. After you drink the hot cocoa.

    d. When the mixture starts to bubble around the edge of the pan.

3. What is another good name for this treat?

    a. "Yummy Winter Drink."

    b. "Milk and Vanilla."

    c. "Boiled Water."

    d. "Drinking Cocoa Powder."

4. A good reason to have an adult help you when you make this treat is that—

    a. hot burners and hot drinks can burn you.

    b. it is more fun to work with someone else.

    c. it takes two people to do all the work.

    d. a child needs help when measuring sugar.

5. The writer probably wrote this recipe to—

    a. tell you what Arturo and Carlos usually do.

    b. warn you to turn off burners.

    c. warn you about cold winters.

    d. tell you how to make hot cocoa.

Peanut Butter Banana Sandwiches

Peanut Butter Banana Sandwiches

Food You Will Need:
4 slices of raisin bread

peanut butter

1 banana

Equipment You Will Need:
toaster

table knife

cutting board

Directions

1. With help from an adult, toast the bread. Use the table knife to spread one side of two pieces with some peanut butter.

2. Peel the banana. Put it on the cutting board. Use the table knife to slice up the banana.

3. Cover each piece of the peanut butter toast with banana slices. Top each sandwich with a plain piece of toast.

4. Put each sandwich on a plate.

5. Throw away the banana peel. Put away the peanut butter and the bread. Wash the cutting board and the table knife.

Makes 2 sandwiches.

Peanut Butter Banana Sandwiches *(cont.)*

Reading Comprehension Questions

After reading the story, answer the questions. Circle the correct answer.

1. The final step in the instructions is to—

    a. wash the cutting board and the table knife.

    b. spread the peanut butter on the toast.

    c. top the toast with banana slices.

    d. eat the sandwiches.

2. What type of tool should you use for this recipe?

    a. knife.

    b. fork.

    c. ruler.

    d. spoon.

3. It's a good idea to have an adult help you with this recipe because—

    a. you might not know where the peanut butter is kept.

    b. you could get burned or cut.

    c. peeling bananas is hard work.

    d. it's more fun to work with someone else.

4. The directions in this passage are about—

    a. mashing bananas with peanut butter to make sandwiches.

    b. how to make peanut butter banana sandwiches.

    c. the invention of peanut butter banana sandwiches.

    d. different ways to use raisin bread.

5. One way to find more ideas like this is to—

    a. watch a program on harvesting peanuts.

    b. make banana bread.

    c. look in the bread section at the store.

    d. look in a kid's cookbook.

> **Directions:** Read this story carefully. When you are completely finished, answer the questions on the next page. Make sure to completely fill in the bubbles

The Model Plane

Gustav was always building model airplanes. Gustav's little brother, Leonard, liked airplanes too! Leonard looked up to his big brother and was always interested whenever Gustav brought a new plane home. So, when Gustav walked in carrying a box, Leonard immediately jumped up to see what his older brother had brought home.

"What kind of plane is this?" Leonard asked.

"This one is a little different from the ones I usually buy. It actually flies," Gustav replied.

"Really flies? How does it work?" Leonard asked.

"Well, you'll have to wait and see," Gustav answered. He tore off the top of the box to reveal a pile of balsa wood parts. Leonard didn't see an airplane—he saw a lot of work. Nevertheless, they pulled the parts from the box and laid out the sheet of directions.

They glued the wings together and fit them through a slot in the body of the plane. Gustav explained that the body was called the fuselage. There was a tail that they glued to the back of the plane and a smaller wing that fit underneath the tail. Gustav said that was called a stabilizer.

Leonard looked at the completed plane. "It just looks like a glider," he said. "You've made those before. They don't fly very well. What's different about this one?" he asked.

"It's not just another glider," said Gustav. "There's one more piece we have to attach to make it work." Gustav took a red plastic propeller and a rubber band out of the box. He fit the propeller over the nose of the plane and connected the rubber band to it. Then he stretched the rubber band to the back of the plane where he looped it on a metal hook.

"Now, it's an airplane," said Gustav. "You see, a plane needs two things to make it fly. It needs thrust-power to pull it through the air." He pointed at the propeller. "A plane also needs lift, which is created when air flows over the wing. If a plane does not have enough thrust, the air will slow it down and it will fall. If a plane does not have enough lift, gravity will pull it down and it will fall."

Gustav walked over to the sliding door that led to their porch. Leonard followed him. Gustav held the plane with one hand and twisted the propeller around several times with the other. Then he handed the plane to his little brother.

"Here, Leonard, you launch it," Gustav said.

Leonard held the plane high in the air and let go. The plane zipped forward and up, moving in a straight line towards the sky. Leonard lost sight of the plane after a few seconds. Gustav picked up his little brother so he could see the plane fly. It was still going!

"I hope it comes back, Gustav. That was a great plane!"

The Model Plane (cont.)

1. What does the propeller do for the plane?

   (a) It gives the plane lift.

   (b) It gives the plane thrust-power.

   (c) It makes the plane look nicer.

   (d) It makes the plane glide smoothly.

2. How does Leonard feel about his older brother?

   (a) He does not like to spend time with him.

   (b) He thinks of him as an airplane pilot.

   (c) He thinks of him as someone he needs to teach.

   (d) He looks up to his older brother.

3. How does Gustav probably feel about his younger brother?

   (a) He is annoyed that Leonard always wants to be with him.

   (b) He thinks of him as an expert on model planes.

   (c) He enjoys spending time with him.

   (d) He thinks of him as too young to understand model planes.

4. When Leonard sees the pile of balsa wood parts, why does the story say that Leonard "didn't see an airplane—he saw a lot of work"?

   (a) Leonard thinks it will be a lot of work to make the wood into an airplane.

   (b) Leonard thinks that planes are impossible to build.

   (c) Leonard thinks the wood is for a model ship instead.

   (d) Leonard thinks he will have to work hard to understand thrust-power.

5. What is the main idea of this story?

   (a) Leonard launches the model plane.

   (b) Gustav and Leonard build and fly a model plane.

   (c) Leonard is excited about the new plane Gustav has brought home.

   (d) Leonard asks Gustav questions about model planes.

Directions: Read this story carefully. When you are completely finished answer the questions on the next page. Make sure to completely fill in the bubbles

The Walrus—A Tool Kit on His Face

Walruses are giant sea mammals. These giants look like their cousins, the seals. Both of these sea mammals have flippers instead of hands. They use the flippers to swim through the water at speeds up to 20 miles an hour. Every walrus also has two important tools that help it live without hands. These tools are its whiskers and its tusks.

Walruses have special whiskers called vibrissae. Unlike normal hair, these whiskers can really feel things. The walruses hunt in deep water. Light from the sun doesn't shine that deep. This means walruses have to find food in the dark. They use their vibrissae to feel for clams and other small creatures to eat.

Walruses have another tool. They have tusks like elephants. They use these tusks in many ways. Walruses live in the arctic where the water is cold. They dive deep in the cold water to hunt for clams. Between dives, they sun themselves to get warm. The only way to get warm is by lying on chunks of sea ice. But walruses can weigh 1,000 pounds. How can these giant animals get out of the water and onto the ice? They use their tusks. They stick their heads out of the water and plant their tusks in the ice like an ice ax. Then they pull themselves out of the water. That takes some pretty strong neck muscles.

Tusks are used for protection, too. Walruses live in large groups. They sit together to keep warm, but sometimes they fight for space. The walrus with the biggest tusks usually wins. The tusks are also useful for chasing off polar bears. Polar bears are good hunters, but the bears usually leave walruses alone because of their tusks.

People used to think that walruses used their tusks to dig for clams. Now people know that this is not true. Walruses fill their mouths with water. Then they squirt the water at the clam. This powerful stream of water moves the sand away from the clam so the walrus can eat it.

Walrus tusks are made out of ivory. People used to hunt walruses for this ivory. Ivory was carved into statues or tools. Today walruses are protected from hunters and get to keep their special tools for themselves.

42

The Walrus—A Tool Kit on His Face *(cont.)*

1 What are tusks used for?

ⓐ Tusks are used to help walruses get onto the ice.

ⓑ They help walruses warm themselves in the sun.

ⓒ They are used to help walruses see underwater.

ⓓ Tusks are used to dig for clams.

2. What do whiskers do?

ⓐ They help the walrus move sand away from clams.

ⓑ They help the walrus swim through the water at a fast speed.

ⓒ They help the walrus feel for clams and other small creatures to eat.

ⓓ They help the walrus fight for space on the ice.

3. The first paragraph answers which of the following questions?

ⓐ Why do walruses fill their mouths with water?

ⓑ How do walruses keep warm?

ⓒ What does a walrus look like?

ⓓ How are walruses like elephants?

4. You can tell that the writer of the passage thinks that walruses are—

ⓐ boring.

ⓑ cute.

ⓒ ugly.

ⓓ interesting.

5. The writer wrote this passage to show that—

ⓐ polar bears usually leave walruses alone.

ⓑ people hunt walruses for their tusks.

ⓒ walruses live in the arctic, where it is very cold.

ⓓ walruses have special tools that help them to live without hands.

Directions: Read this story carefully. When you are completely finished, answer the questions on the next page. Make sure to completely fill in the bubbles

Growing Sunflowers

Suki and Miko were glad to see the warm spring sun. They were eager to plant the seeds that Grandfather had given them. Grandfather told them they should plant some of the seeds indoors and some outdoors so the flowers would bloom at different times. Grandfather carefully prepared the following planting directions for them.

Prado Red

Prado Red is a new type of sunflower. It is very pretty in garden flower beds. It also provides long-lasting flowers for bouquets. The four-foot tall plants branch off near the ground. Each stem is crowned with deep, red flowers.

For Best Results

1. When the weather has warmed up (both day and night), plant the seeds. Sow the seeds $1/2$ inch deep in the soil. They will do best in a spot that gets lots of sun.

2. As soon as the seeds are planted in the soil, cover them with netting or plastic berry baskets to protect them from birds. Remove the netting or baskets before the plants get too big.

3. Remember to keep the soil from drying out until the seeds begin to sprout. This should take place in five to ten days.

4. Once they have sprouted, dig up the seedlings and plant them again so that they are about 10 to 12 inches apart.

For Early Blooms

1. Seeds can be planted indoors in a warm place. Plant them one or two weeks before the last day of frost. Plant the seeds in separate pots of seed-starting mix.

2. When the seedlings appear, put the pots in an area where they will enjoy strong light.

3. When the weather has warmed up and the plants are three to four inches tall, get the plants used to being outdoors by placing them outside for short periods of time.

4. When the plants are used to being outside, plant them in the garden.

Growing Sunflowers *(cont.)*

1. Why did Grandfather say to plant some seeds indoors and others outdoors?

    ⓐ So the girls could enjoy the flowers inside and outside.

    ⓑ So all the flowers would not bloom at once.

    ⓒ Because the seeds outside may be eaten by birds.

    ⓓ Because Grandfather gave them too many seeds for one place.

2. Which of the following is true of the sunflower called Prado Red?

    ⓐ It is larger than other sunflowers.

    ⓑ It is easy to grow all year long.

    ⓒ It is difficult to replant.

    ⓓ It is good in bouquets.

3. What is the main idea of the section called "For Early Blooms?"

    ⓐ To explain that plants get used to the outdoors by being placed outside for short periods of time.

    ⓑ To tell gardeners how to thin out their plants.

    ⓒ To tell about a new type of sunflower.

    ⓓ To show that outdoor plants can be started early indoors.

4. Which of the following is an opinion in these directions?

    ⓐ Prado Red is very pretty in garden flower beds.

    ⓑ Each stem is crowned with deep, red flowers.

    ⓒ The four-foot tall plants branch off near the ground.

    ⓓ Prado Red is a new type of sunflower.

5. You can tell from this passage that—

    ⓐ Prado Red flowers wilt quickly.

    ⓑ Suki and Miko miss the winter snow.

    ⓒ Grandfather is an experienced gardener.

    ⓓ Prado Red seeds take a month to sprout.

Practice Answer Sheet

This sheet may be reproduced and used with the reading comprehension questions. Each box can be used with one story. Using the answer sheets with the stories and questions gives extra practice in test preparation.

Page 5	Page 7	Page 9
1. ⓐ ⓑ ⓒ ⓓ	1. ⓐ ⓑ ⓒ ⓓ	1. ⓐ ⓑ ⓒ ⓓ
2. ⓐ ⓑ ⓒ ⓓ	2. ⓐ ⓑ ⓒ ⓓ	2. ⓐ ⓑ ⓒ ⓓ
3. ⓐ ⓑ ⓒ ⓓ	3. ⓐ ⓑ ⓒ ⓓ	3. ⓐ ⓑ ⓒ ⓓ
4. ⓐ ⓑ ⓒ ⓓ	4. ⓐ ⓑ ⓒ ⓓ	4. ⓐ ⓑ ⓒ ⓓ
5. ⓐ ⓑ ⓒ ⓓ	5. ⓐ ⓑ ⓒ ⓓ	5. ⓐ ⓑ ⓒ ⓓ
Page 11	**Page 13**	**Page 15**
1. ⓐ ⓑ ⓒ ⓓ	1. ⓐ ⓑ ⓒ ⓓ	1. ⓐ ⓑ ⓒ ⓓ
2. ⓐ ⓑ ⓒ ⓓ	2. ⓐ ⓑ ⓒ ⓓ	2. ⓐ ⓑ ⓒ ⓓ
3. ⓐ ⓑ ⓒ ⓓ	3. ⓐ ⓑ ⓒ ⓓ	3. ⓐ ⓑ ⓒ ⓓ
4. ⓐ ⓑ ⓒ ⓓ	4. ⓐ ⓑ ⓒ ⓓ	4. ⓐ ⓑ ⓒ ⓓ
5. ⓐ ⓑ ⓒ ⓓ	5. ⓐ ⓑ ⓒ ⓓ	5. ⓐ ⓑ ⓒ ⓓ
Page 17	**Page 19**	**Page 21**
1. ⓐ ⓑ ⓒ ⓓ	1. ⓐ ⓑ ⓒ ⓓ	1. ⓐ ⓑ ⓒ ⓓ
2. ⓐ ⓑ ⓒ ⓓ	2. ⓐ ⓑ ⓒ ⓓ	2. ⓐ ⓑ ⓒ ⓓ
3. ⓐ ⓑ ⓒ ⓓ	3. ⓐ ⓑ ⓒ ⓓ	3. ⓐ ⓑ ⓒ ⓓ
4. ⓐ ⓑ ⓒ ⓓ	4. ⓐ ⓑ ⓒ ⓓ	4. ⓐ ⓑ ⓒ ⓓ
5. ⓐ ⓑ ⓒ ⓓ	5. ⓐ ⓑ ⓒ ⓓ	5. ⓐ ⓑ ⓒ ⓓ

Practice Answer Sheet *(cont.)*

Page 23	Page 25	Page 27
1. (a) (b) (c) (d)	1. (a) (b) (c) (d)	1. (a) (b) (c) (d)
2. (a) (b) (c) (d)	2. (a) (b) (c) (d)	2. (a) (b) (c) (d)
3. (a) (b) (c) (d)	3. (a) (b) (c) (d)	3. (a) (b) (c) (d)
4. (a) (b) (c) (d)	4. (a) (b) (c) (d)	4. (a) (b) (c) (d)
5. (a) (b) (c) (d)	5. (a) (b) (c) (d)	5. (a) (b) (c) (d)
Page 29	**Page 31**	**Page 33**
1. (a) (b) (c) (d)	1. (a) (b) (c) (d)	1. (a) (b) (c) (d)
2. (a) (b) (c) (d)	2. (a) (b) (c) (d)	2. (a) (b) (c) (d)
3. (a) (b) (c) (d)	3. (a) (b) (c) (d)	3. (a) (b) (c) (d)
4. (a) (b) (c) (d)	4. (a) (b) (c) (d)	4. (a) (b) (c) (d)
5. (a) (b) (c) (d)	5. (a) (b) (c) (d)	5. (a) (b) (c) (d)
Page 35	**Page 37**	**Page 39**
1. (a) (b) (c) (d)	1. (a) (b) (c) (d)	1. (a) (b) (c) (d)
2. (a) (b) (c) (d)	2. (a) (b) (c) (d)	2. (a) (b) (c) (d)
3. (a) (b) (c) (d)	3. (a) (b) (c) (d)	3. (a) (b) (c) (d)
4. (a) (b) (c) (d)	4. (a) (b) (c) (d)	4. (a) (b) (c) (d)
5. (a) (b) (c) (d)	5. (a) (b) (c) (d)	5. (a) (b) (c) (d)

Answer Key

Happy Birthday, page 5
1. c
2. a
3. a
4. c
5. b

Help Our Baby!, page 7
1. b
2. d
3. d
4. a
5. c

The Fawn, page 9
1. b
2. d
3. a
4. b
5. a

Mike the Cat, page 11
1. b
2. a
3. a
4. d
5. a

The Wood Carver, page 13
1. d
2. a
3. b
4. a
5. b

Square Dancing Llamas, page 15
1. b
2. c
3. d
4. c
5. a

Shirley Temple, page 17
1. b
2. a
3. d
4. c
5. b

Sky Pioneers, page 19
1. b
2. c
3. d
4. b
5. b

To the Moon!, page 21
1. c
2. b
3. b
4. c
5. c

The Moth Named for the Moon, page 23
1. b
2. c
3. a
4. d
5. c

Horses with Pull, page 25
1. d
2. c
3. a
4. c
5. b

Weird Weather, page 27
1. a
2. a
3. a
4. a
5. c

How to Live in Death Valley, page 29
1. c
2. c
3. c
4. c
5. b

Rainbow Soup, page 31
1. b
2. c
3. c
4. b
5. d

Checking Out Books page 33
1. c
2. a
3. c
4. a
5. c

Applesauce, page 35
1. a
2. d
3. a
4. a
5. c

Hot Cocoa, page 37
1. b
2. d
3. a
4. a
5. d

Peanut Butter Banana Sandwiches, page 39
1. a
2. a
3. b
4. b
5. d

The Model Plane, page 41
1. b
2. d
3. c
4. a
5. b

The Walrus—A Tool Kit on His Face, page 43
1. a
2. c
3. c
4. d
5. d

Growing Sunflowers, page 45
1. b
2. d
3. d
4. a
5. c